HEAVEN THROUGH THE EYES OF

KOSHKA THE VICARAGE CAT

by

The Reverend John Foden Lee A.K.C.

PUBLISHER
BARBARA C.LEE

PRINTED BY THE BASINGSTOKE PRESS.

ISBN 0-9531444-1-0.

First published September 2001
Reprinted May 2002

INTRODUCTION

KOSHKA, "THE VICARAGE CAT", is a story of how that illusive place, which we call "Heaven", can be found in spite of hostile circumstances and conditions. Barbara faced a house-bound future with the disabling pains of rheumatoid arthritis and our daughter, Joanna, was killed aged 26 in a road accident on 14th October 1992 in the East End of London. Paul and Simon, her small children, also came to live at the Vicarage and Koshka was very important for them. Koshka managed to live to see old age, in spite of the menace of the internal combustion engine, and saw us through the gates of retirement to Surrey and beyond.

I dedicate this little book to her and all other God's creatures, great and small, who have met untimely deaths on the road.

My special thanks to Liz Taylor who has given me so much of her time and skills on preparing this book for the printers and Dr. Ann Barrington for keeping me on the grammatical "straight and narrow"!

John Foden Lee
14th October 2001

CONTENTS

PHOTOGRAPHS

CARTOON ILLUSTRATIONS

by
Stephen Goddard of Godalming

CHAPTER 1

IN PRAISE OF VICARAGE CATS

TIMMY was our first Vicarage cat, a ginger tom whose territorial oversight and appearance made him – in the eyes of many – Bishop among cats; I am sure we should have addressed him as the 'Right Reverend Timothy Lee'.

Humans are said to have souls and cats not, but experience leads me to believe the converse; cats have souls, humans often seem to have lost theirs!

The Right Reverend Timothy, as a kitten slid down the slide on his bottom, taking his turn with the children. He even took his place in the circle for 'pass the parcel', while as an adult he attended Parochial Church Council Meetings and Wine and Cheese gatherings at Erlestoke Vicarage.

Timmy opening the Vicarage Door

Timmy could open the huge doors by stretching up four feet to spring latches, scaring strangers by his 'rap, tap, tap' on the large iron door rings to announce his arrival as if part of an episcopal ceremony.

He did not wait for you to bend down to stroke him, but stood on his hind legs showing his pure white throat and rubbed his fine head against your hand. He lived seven magnificent years, when he used to watch me gardening with an interest far more all–knowing than that of any other creature.

He was killed on the Jubilee celebrations with two other cats on the bottom road, caught out by the sudden influx of convoys of cars which raced in drunken pursuit of the bonfires along the narrow roads.

Timmy was buried in the Vicarage garden in the red, white and blue in which he had been fittingly wrapped by the parishioner who found him: another sacrifice to our folly.

'Honey' by name, 'Honey' by nature was the little

Timmy, the Episcopal cat, arriving at a
Parochial Church Council Meeting

handicapped cat which replaced 'the Bishop'. He had been spotted as a ginger ball of fluff, playing with the other cats in a farmhouse and farmyard barns.

Perhaps he was just as clever as his superior predecessor, for not only did he not mature to full size, he could not 'meow'. Have you ever seen a cat try to 'meow' which cannot do so?

Honey tried to the point of turning himself into one of Hiawatha's mittens, 'made them with the fur side inside! Made them with the skinside outside'. His brave attempts to meow seemed destined to achieve such an undesirable result! Honey put up with life quietly and humbly and endured people in a saint-like way. The mighty traffic of the Street claimed this poor three year old fellow, who possibly would have been no match for the high society of feline Seend!

'Lucky' was given his name as an omen for Karen's O-

Levels. He was too small to leave behind on holiday so we took him to Scotland with us. Jet black, we led this diminutive Don Quixote around on a leash sporting a bell and tartan collar of the McPussy Clan! Lucky Lee was famous for arching his kitten back and tilting at car wheels as if to take on the whole Goliath armour-clad human world.

Lucky survived the Street to die of a kidney infection at the age of four.

Lucky Lee was famous for arching his kitten back

Buddhists hold the cat – so I have been told – as the only perfect creature and break their tails to prevent them retaining their perfection and rivalling the divine. We need not do such things in the West, as we maim them mostly with the motor car.

'Sam' was meant to be another boy cat, but there seemed to be something of importance missing and she was our first female feline.

In the wild the she-cat is a splendid sister, daughter, aunt and mother; so it was with 'Sam'. Sometimes I would lie on the floor with a bad back and a sense of sadness and burden of the world when a little tongue would lick me; here was a sense of a touch from the real world which communicates care, love and the spirit of One whose life is rooted in the unseen durable world of eternity.

Sam disappeared up the stairs to the airing cupboard, to give birth to two kittens 'Black and White'. The cleanliness and attention of the young mother was wonderful and she moved the kittens from their elevated maternity ward so that they would not fall and hurt themselves.

She moved her kittens to Joanna's bedroom and sat on her lap with the incredible gesture 'you don't mind do you, sister, we've moved in with you!

I know that we must not endanger human life by too much concern for animals on the highway, but it could be that a greater deference for both creature and human beings might be essential for the saving of their mutual eternal souls.

Sam aged one, was killed 26 June 1985 on Seend High Street by a lorry travelling at 60mph, leaving two four week orphans 'Black and White'. They have yet to be christened and given their proper names.

Joanna and the Church of Holy Cross, Seend. 1986
Preparing to move to Derby with Koshka and Sheba

Surrogate Motherhood

Koshka & Sheba in Derby

Barbara & Koshka

CHAPTER 2

KOSHKA AND SHEBA

A large flesh-eating feline suddenly alarmed the Street; it was a black sleek Jaguar of the automobile kind! A passing boy scout could not suppress his feelings of horror as the expensive limousine screeched to an abrupt halt. Another cat lost its ninth life! A few weeks later Lavinia Thorpe, an equally striking figure, raced along the Street remonstrating with a speeding juggernaut which in contempt of the Highway Code squashed our cat, 'Sammy' into the unforgiving gutter. Liz Futter, our Bulkington Church Treasurer, happened to be passing in the wake of this tragedy. Ever caring and thoughtful, Liz dismounted her bicycle and placed Sammy's remains in a plastic bag by the Vicarage door with the merciful epitaph 'DO NOT LOOK INSIDE'!

'BLACK and WHITE' Sammy's kittens were one month old when they were orphaned. Barbara had to become their surrogate mother. Cows milk is not suitable initially for human babies, nor is it suitable for diminutive kittens. Barbara with a doll-sized feeding bottle, a syringe, weaned her new daughters with the powdered cat's milk prescribed by the vet with plenty of T.L.C. It was June and the kittens took up their summer residence at the bottom of the garden, safely hidden under a large bay tree. Sammy's motherhood, sadly curtailed as it was, was long enough to impart to Black some essential lessons, Black was the older and bigger kitten and had the submissive attentiveness of a nun in her noviciate; her white apron-like front underlined in her habit her calling to obedience.

White was different; unteachable and quite unable to sit still. Sammy pinned her down to the carpet with a firm paw to end what would have been interminable fussiness or 'puss-i-ness'. After Sammy's death Black carried on her discipline and corporal restraints.

Barbara named 'Black', Sheba, because like the Queen of the South she was dignified with a regal aloofness; she was very athletic and had a spirit which was in touch with a higher realm than the ordinary world we euphemistically call 'human'. I thought of her as a highly sophisticated left-wing philosopher, while 'White' I nicknamed 'S.D.P (Silly Daft Pussy). Eventually I called her Koshka, the female form of KOT the Russian for a tom cat. The diminutive 'Koshechka' was the better name by which I remember her. Our son-in-law Howard was the first to favour Koshka; he saw her markings as endearing and delightful. Her fur was long – but not too long; her face had an icon-like beauty in the only real sense of that beautiful word!

But in contrast with Sheba's athletic elegance Koshka had a plumpish roundness accentuated by half-length black stockings as if her Creator meant her to be tinged with the comical and humorous. Her paws were covered by snow-white soft fur gloves.

The kittens grew up in the magical world of Seend Vicarage for the first eight months of their lives before we moved to St. Paul's Vicarage in Derby.

Koshka & Sheba in the security of Seend Vicarage
by the Bay tree

Cats are bad, bad passengers and not surprisingly have more than hostile distrust of the internal combustion engine; they see it as "machina vera diaboli". The German phrase 'es ist besser zu Fusse zu gehen' (it is better to walk) is incontrovertible from any cats point of view. Hector Hugo Munro in his 'The Achievement of the Cat' writes "confront a child, a puppy and a kitten with sudden danger; the child will turn instinctively for assistance, the puppy will grovel in abject submission to the impending visitation, the kitten will brace its tiny body for frantic resistance". As I have said Lucky Lee had shown his hostility and courage when any vehicle approached him by arching his kitten back like a folded hinge and hissing and threatening wheels with whiskers and fur standing on end. Timmy, the Bishop, turned into a caged tiger when put into a motor car and his spot of courting was abruptly terminated on Hampton's farm. Sheba's nun-like self-control never changed as we motored up the Fosse Way to Derby whilst Koshka punctuated the journey by being indiscreetly sick at Moreton-in-the-Marsh.

Joanna travelled with her kitten nieces in our Fiat Panda and it is intriguing to observe and compare how kittens and children take stock of their new home and environs – they immediately take everything in. They notice secure and comfortable areas which they claim as their own and always have an eye for bolt-holes and any potential means of escape. Our new vicarage had two single beds in the spare room of which Sheba and Koshka immediately, took charge.

It was uncanny on our arrival in Derby to find the eight

months old kittens stretched out full length on separate beds with an air of contentment with an expression of "This will do for us, Thank-you-very-much" !

The Coach and Horses, Derby

CHAPTER 3

CAT-NAPPED

Chester Green is built on the foundations of Derventio ancient Derby and the Coach & Horses stands conveniently opposite the Vicarage. From the inside on the window ledge I could see silhouetted against the night sky two kittens patiently awaiting my home-coming. A clergyman does not need such "tell-tales" fixing his whereabouts!

Rudyard Kipling in his famous 'The Cat that walked by Himself' describes why men from earliest times are hostile to cats: 'Then the Man threw his two boots and his little stone axe (that makes three) at the Cat, and the Cat ran out of the cave and the Dog chased him up the tree, and from that day to this, Best Beloved, three proper men out of five will always throw things at a Cat whenever they meet him, and all proper dogs will chase him up a tree. But the Cat keeps his side of the bargain too. He will kill mice and he will be kind to Babies when he is in the house, as long as they do not pull his tail too hard. But when he has done that, and between times, he is the Cat that walks by himself and all places are alike to him, and if you look out at nights you can see him waving his wild tail and walking by his wild lone – just the same as before'.

Human history in part is a sad story of how we try to dominate others and control everything; we have the mistaken idea that God is made in our image and not the other way round. Cats in particular resist this arrogant piece of theology and all attempts of domestication; they challenge all the boundaries that so easily flow from this wrong-headedness. Sheba was at cross purposes with me in such delicate matters of outdoor toilets and toiletry. She could not grasp the logic that says the most carefully graded seed-beds are "OUT OF BOUNDS" - "STRICTLY FORBIDDEN" - TRESPASSERS WILL BE P-U-R-R-SECUTED" !!! Sheba could not grasp why such ideal areas were taboo and were even perilous to contemplate! And why the hand that fed could be so readily raised against her. Whenever Sheba selected such a prime site in the middle of the garden the heavens opened and it rained volleys of earth but Koshka's toiletry was undisturbed beneath

Sheba carries out an experiment in matters toiletry

the young apple tree which was a gift from the parishioners of Bulkington. When this confrontation was at its highest, Sheba, it seemed, carried out an experiment to understand why she alone was singled out for such flak. With the greatest deliberation she scratched a hole in the most exposed seed-bed and retreated at a safe distance to the path by the rhubarb patch. For once Koshka was attentive and whatever was communicated had the effect that she immediately proceeded to the ear-marked spot! Of course the experiment only proved my unreasonableness and in the case of punishment there was no favouritism or special treatment.

Cats have many enemies, especially gardeners and bird lovers. When Barbara faced a future of being house-bound, I decided to make the Vicarage garden part of paradise. One thing I did was to place a large turkey leg in a small sugar bowl to encourage and welcome wild life into the middle of Derby. As expected the turkey leg went missing and the recipient left a fair sized 'plopsy' as a 'Thank-you' note. I wondered who could have been my bizarre visitor? So I asked the ladies of the Precision Casting Facility at Rolls-Royce what creature could have managed such a trick?

Some said it might have been a hedgehog, others a squirrel, while others suggested it might have been a fox. One person opted for a cat. "Cats always dig holes in the garden", insisted a voice in the background "my Dad saw a cat digging a hole". "That's not unusual", responded a lassie, looking up from the wax blade on which she was applying some finishing touches. "That's not strange, cats always do that!" "Oh yes it was . . . . this cat was Irish" said my Dad, "it was carrying a shovel!"

O'Catty the Irish Cat

Sheba continued to teach Koshka the art of survival and how to cope – hunting was the last lesson. She caught a bird or an insect and passed it on to her sister for educational purposes; like all good mothers she went without for her dependant. Koshka always ate first and growled with contentment and a menacing warning to keep well away. It was amusing in later life to watch Koshka eyeing plump pigeons eating fearlessly on the lawn; her jaw would drop and her lip trembled as she muttered in 'cat-ese' with the same threatening growl what she would do to them if there were no patio window in her way.

Sheba suddenly went missing. My heart sank when a parishioner told me that a 'black cat was seen dead on the Old Chester Road and was taken away in a dust cart!' I had given Sheba up as dead when, after three days of searching, out of the mists of early morning walked our super cat. In great excitement I ran home and announced to the Bishop of Repton and Paddy our guests, that I had seen Sheba, "she had risen from the dead!" They both gave me pitying looks of incredulity. The real truth was that Sheba had been 'cat-napped' by a Methodist. The cat that had left the parish so ignominiously in the dust cart had been hers and in the ecumenical spirit that prevailed in this part of Derby the 'cat-napper' said, "it is only the Vicars cat, he won't miss it, he has two!"

It reminded me of the cat that went missing in Bristol and then turned up at Temple Meads Station after two years when its 'cat-napper' arbitrarily moved house. It certainly had missed the train. Sheba returned home when her 'cat-napper' locked her out in the snow but she went missing again when the better weather came. A few months later when Barbara was collecting Christian Aid Envelopes she caught sight of Sheba sitting in the woman's armchair. "That's my cat!" she exclaimed. The 'cat napper' unashamedly admitted that she knew it was the Vicarage cat! Barbara told the old lady that Sheba could continue in her new home providing at the end of the day – if necessary- she would be returned home to the Vicarage. But sadly the 'cat-napper' went into a home and we were told in a roundabout way through the representative of the Cats League that Sheba had also gone 'to a good home!'

I feared the worst as I recalled the euphemistic words of the old hymn, "There's a home for little children above the bright blue skies".

If Paradise had been lost then we would find it a home!

CHAPTER 4

KOSHKA

Barbara was becoming increasingly ill with a most painful debilitating form of arthritis; she faced daily the possibility of becoming 'housebound' or as the Americans put it a 'SHUT IN'. I decided that St. Paul's Vicarage should be like a monastery garden of the Greek Orthodox Church or like St. Catherine's in Cable Street in that grim part of the East End of London – If Paradise had been lost then we would find it at home!

No sooner than I had started to clear the ground than heavenly visitors began to appear. The easy-to-grow buddleia attracted butterflies from thousands of miles away – red admirals with their two red bands on each pair of wings; the mottled tortoiseshells and the peacocks. The newly-dug pond with its cascade and water lilies was soon filled with healthy red and orange goldfish. The primeval dragonfly and its more dainty cousins, green and blue damsel flies, settled with their delicate wings folded like ballerinas as they rested in the rockery waterside plants. A mallard duck with his mate thought the spot attractive enough to grace us with his presence, accompanied closely by an exotic mandarin duck. In this microcosm of Eden Koshka was the star performer on the stage in this Divine Comedy. In the middle of our garden, like the one in Genesis – there was 'The Tree of Life'! A magnificent ancient pear tree which leant with old age over a Roman well with its richly coloured bark like the brownish-red skin of an antediluvian crocodile. In the Springtime it was curtained with heavy white blossoms which kissed the lawn to awake and reveal the seasons in the calendar of miracle and magic!

One afternoon I was abruptly distracted from watching television by a sudden excitement and a most invasive commotion in the pear tree; there were dozens of twittering small birds filling the bare branches and twigs with their colourful plumage and busy presence. One half of the tree was momentarily occupied by long-tailed tits with their broad black stripes above their eyes and strong pinkish-buff on their rumps;

on the other half Europe's smallest bird (the crested wren) simultaneously paused in flight!

I walked to the patio window and a voice said to me " Look outside!"

There is much more that is interesting happening outside, you are wasting your time looking at that!"

The point was made by the dreadful deep truth, "you are not only wasting your time, you are wasting my time!"

Koshka's freedom to come and go as she pleased was blocked by the flimsiest kitchen door. This obstacle was removed by a stroke of good fortune when Derby Police broke it down to arrest a thirteen year old boy who had taken over the Vicarage by climbing through an upstairs window. The police had surrounded the house and laid siege to the youth who threatened to shoot his assailants with my bow and arrow through the letter box. This event caused great interest in the Coach & Horses and on our homecoming we were welcomed by an atmosphere of bemused amusement. Barbara and I crossed Old Chester Road to see what the fuss was all about. The below-standard door was smashed, and patched up as if it had gone fifteen rounds with Mike Tyson. The constabulary replaced it out of police funds but with the addition of a cat flap! In a manner of speaking Koshka had been given the key to the door, thus gaining complete access to house and garden.

Koshka's happiness continued in the blissful problem-free circumstances apart from getting stuck on the roof on one occasion and on another accidentally being imprisoned in the attic of the Old Vicarage. It was particularly funny to see her stalking with total motionless seriousness as if with a placard advertising "I'm invisible" or "I'm not here!" Had we had snow all the year round or had she been born in the Arctic then her white fur would have camouflaged her well. One of the squirrels she hunted was a Jerry-like cartoon character who teased her unmercifully; he let her get within a whisker then frustrated her brave attempts to catch him by accelerating to the safety of the fence or the trees. On a few occasions when Koshka had retired exhausted to the front room he would tap on the patio window as if to say, 'Ya boo! Come and catch me if you can!" On other occasions a family of young squirrels tantalised and tempted in displays of breath-taking gymnastics.

In Springtime a pair of crows were regular visitors and joined in the sport. They built their nest in the large horse-chestnut tree bordering on Darley Abbey Park; they too had to protect their property from the attacks of these marauding nimble cheeky rodents. Koshka's excitement was uncontainable while the crows annoyance was at its limit; these parent crows nose-bombed the trapped squirrel as it took cover in the adequate foliage of the pear tree. Koshka cut off the squirrel's only way of escape by positioning herself at the foot of the tree. The game always ended with the invincible squirrel escaping on the blind side of the tree having engaged the cat in 'peepo' or a prolonged game of hide and seek. Thus concluding another interlude in another of the garden's variety shows!

Vicarage Visitors

Ben with the Favourite Toy

Paul takes to Vicarage Gardening

A Heavenly Smile from Harriet

Simon a Gifted Sportsman

CHAPTER 5

THE INTERNAL INFERNAL COMBUSTION ENGINE

Every member of the congregation of St. Paul's was given a piece of a circular jigsaw puzzle and asked to imagine the picture which all the bits together would make. On the front of its box there was a completed scene of part of Paradise; exotic plants, a tiger, other animals and colourful birds which reflected a primeval state of being – there were no humans. Although we are undoubtedly the most disruptive force on this planet – and the cause of its disruption – we are the vital ingredient for its ultimate healing in the scheme of things. Oscar Wilde made this point most movingly in his 'The Selfish Giant'; blessedness is where children play and where the joyful voices of God's little ones are heard.

Every Spring Bank Holiday at Rogationtide the Roman well in the Vicarage garden was dressed with flowers and the local population was encouraged to ponder a mosaic depicting a scene from the Old or New Testamental times. This human activity attracted the animals to join in the festivities; the collages of barley, maize, sunflower seeds, nuts and other edible titbits were open invitations for birds and squirrels to be present. Initially animals flee little people but under the right conditions and circumstances little children enhance the magic and miracle of heaven.

Ben held Koshka most awkwardly as he rode his mother's favourite toy, a red horse, round the garden paths; Koshka did not struggle or complain. In this, happiness was somehow complete. Heaven is where and when all things have found their place and are occupied. Ben was never more pre-occupied than when he could get his arm full-length up or down a drain-pipe. While Ben was at home in Bristol he was present in spirit.

"I miss you Ben, I don't see you much these days" I said "Do you miss Granddad?"
"No" the four year old replied in a matter-of-fact way.

"He will kill mice and he will be kind to babies ....
as long as they do not pull his tail too hard."

The Roman Well and the Vicarage Garden

"Why is that?" I asked, mildly wounded.

"I have a magic eye. I can see Granddad whenever I want to" replied the child "And I have magic lips and I can tell Granddad I love him whenever I want to!"

Harriet, Ben's younger sister, had her place too in the garden. She also was part of Koshka's extended family. Joanna – as daughters do – came home on regular visits with two most lovely and loveable little boys – Paul David and Simon Peter. Rudyard Kipling when writing about the cat said "He will be kind to babies when he is in the house, as long as they do not pull his tail too hard". That was most certainly true in Paul and Simon's relationship with Koshka. Joanna – like Sammy – was a very good and natural mother. A neighbour watched her taking the children to playschool in the snow. "She loved those boys so much!" she said. "Paul was in the pushchair while she carried Simon on her shoulders, flying-angel style!".

It is not until people are seriously ill that you realise that your furniture is made for looks rather than for comfort. The Vicarage inside was suddenly dramatically changed; chairs and bed were heightened, my study became a bedroom and the downstairs toilet became a shower. Railings and handles were fixed in strategic places and there was the arrival of the wheelchair.

Many people suffer from arthritis and some have faith in copper bracelets or cod liver oil to work such miracles of healing, but those who really suffer know that such superstitious piety is only a mockery for their excruciating pains. Barbara's bravery and character on the other hand were really effective antidotes in her fight against this most pernicious and disabling disease.

On the 14th October 1992 we were waiting at Birmingham International Airport for our flight to Rhodes. Barbara was in her wheelchair and our names were called out on the tannoy; we thought that we were being called to board the aeroplane. Instead it was to receive the message from Karen and Howard that Joanna had been killed at 11:30am crossing the road on Pritchard Street going to work in the East End of London. Howard gave the sound advice which is imperative on such an occasion "Don't drive!" Cathy Hill, the Duty Terminal Manager said the Airport would do whatever was required.

We decided to take a taxi to Clive and Priscilla's home, our friends in North London to be with Philip, Paul and Simon. To stay in an hotel in Birmingham would mean that we would have just walked the floorboards. The drive to London was also long and the night seemed to be an interminable nightmare.

We slept very briefly in the small hours in Clive and Priscilla's bed. Under different circumstances we would have expected a nocturnal visitor. Joanna and Karen in the first years of their lives had been regular visitors to the parental bed. As a parent when a small person joins you in bed you instinctively move over with the minimum of disturbance to prevent sleep-walking from erupting into total awakeness! Half-awake and half-asleep I felt small feet, tiny hands and be-nappied bottom. I said to Barbara, "There is a small child in bed with us!" She thought that I was hallucinating. Then we both simultaneously woke up to the reality that the little visitor was William, Clive and Priscilla's three year old son who knew nothing of our arrival.

I accepted the fact that sleep had eluded me but my head was filled with a poem which I instantly wrote down:-

William. "A Visitation"

> Jesus came to bed with me
> I felt him at my side
> A little boy who took my place
> For he knew how I cried
> My hand touched a sleeping child
> I asked who could it be?
> It was the Lord of Life
> (He said) who sought to comfort me
> He said I speak in many ways
> But none so crystal clear
> As in guise of a sleeping child
> For Bethlehem is here.

I watched the face of the fair-haired lad

Which measured all our grief.

It showed how deeply he was sad

Who hung beside the thief.

It promised sunshine must break through

The veil that covers light

For without such a kindly shroud

The world would be too bright

In that calm face I saw a maid

The mother of our Lord

In whose womb was the empty tomb

The hope of everyone.

CHAPTER 6
CHRISTMAS

Every year I have said, "This is the best yet!" How could I say it of Christmas 1992?" Then Joanna's death showed me as I had never seen before that we are surrounded by an ocean of invisible and inarticulated love. It gave many the opportunity to show that they cared; I experienced the love that was born at Christmas-time to make it possible for us to cope and be changed. It was as Wordsworth wrote in his pastoral poem, Michael, when the shepherd lost his only son Luke in the big city:

"There is a comfort in the strength of love;
'twill make a thing endurable, which else
Would overset the brain or break the heart:"

The love that was poured out was not directed at me for myself but that it might be shared with those around me – in particular with Paul and Simon, Joanna's children

Philip, Joanna's husband, had collapsed as a result of the accident and the Social Services had arranged for me to pick up the two little boys at Scratchwood Services on the M1.

Paul was just five and Simon was only three.

Paul had opted to go to Granddad, **"He has a pond with a frog in it!"** he said.

As Paul wanted to see a rugby match we stopped off on the Welford Road to see Northampton Saints play Leicester Tigers on our way to see Grandma in the Royal Infirmary. Simon asked, "Are you dead like Mummy, is this heaven?" Barbara showed Simon her leg and told him that hospitals make people better and that hospitals could not make Mummy better. Paul concluded, "If you are killed they can't make you better!"

The next day, Sunday, required my utmost organising skills. After bathing, dressing and giving the boys breakfast I had to celebrate Holy Communion, preach and ensure everything worked happily and harmoniously. I sat Simon with Hazel Moore with a jigsaw and a packet of sweets and I grasped Paul's hand tightly to make certain he was a model altar boy – he, too, was rewarded with a packet of sweets and a jigsaw and sat on the large red carpet during the sermon.

During the first week that Paul and Simon were with us, Simon pulled the large curtains down in front of the patio windows and Koshka also met with an accident. I had freshly mopped the white-tiled kitchen floor, when I spotted tracks of deep red pools of blood which led me to Koshka who had hidden herself under the leaves of the large round table. Something or someone had torn off her tiny chin and part of her tongue was missing. Paul summed up the situation with the words, "We don't want any more members of our family to die!"

We took Koshka to the vet on the Kedleston Road, Derby and Barbara confided in the nurse with the words, "My daughter has been killed. I don't want my cat to die!"

It was Koshka's turn to be in hospital for ten days. The vets amazing skill in wiring up her jaw inspired confidence and trust. All the feeding tubes were removed and she came home wearing a large conical collar. Instead of the tubes she wore a supplementary baby's bib which gave a hint of the comical – especially when at the first opportunity she dashed out of the open kitchen door up the pear tree! She was back in the entertainment business! The vets brilliant surgery was matched by his generosity and kindness, for he reduced the bill by eighty pounds when the nurse passed on Barbara's sad words.

A friend came to stay for a short time at the Vicarage. We were driving in the Peak District when we both noticed simultaneously feathers sticking up out of the grass verge. The road was very dangerous and it was not possible to stop on the double yellow lines which followed the sweeping bends. My curiosity got the better of me and I stopped to go back to investigate. I lifted a tawny owl out of the long grass. The bird was magnificent and beautiful and unmarked, like Joanna had been. Barbara persuaded me to leave the owl where I had found it. I told Paul about the incident and he mildly scolded Barbara and said "you did wrong Grandma! Granddad should have brought the owl home and we could have given it a proper burial!"

Death on the Road

On the following day in the same vicinity in similar conditions I noticed an unusual bird in the middle of the road; its feathers glistened in the heavy rain. Paul was with us this time as I held the tiny bird in the palm of my hand. It wore a red cap and was barred on its back; it was perfect in every detail apart from the absence of that mysterious quality we call 'Life'. It had been a lesser-spotted woodpecker. Somehow, someone was drawing my attention to how we sacrifice to the automobile the dearest and most beautiful of creatures without even the dignity of a primitive ritual!

In subsequent months Paul and Simon were so quiet in church that the congregation and I forgot that they were with us until Paul quietly appeared in the middle of the sermon and whispered as he slipped his little hand in mine in the middle of the sermon, "Tell them about the owl, Granddad!"

Koshka had to share her life with Paul and Simon for nine months and was a very important member of the family. As Sammy had a special relationship with Joanna, So Koshka bonded with the two boys – she was very important in their lives. They could not grasp, however, that Barbara considered herself as Koshka's "Mummy" while they remained simply grandchildren.

When it was time to kiss "Goodnight", Simon, although he was initially unable to show his affections to Grandma, always gave Koshka a kiss, who was in her usual place sitting on Grandma's knee.

Simon and Paul

CHAPTER 7

NEIGHBOURS FROM HELL

When we make our homes heaven, then we inevitably invite harassment from Hell; our microcosmic paradise becomes a honey pot to a swarm of wasps. The garage owner next door ringed his forecourt with a tannoy system and pointed a loud hailer menacingly over the Vicarage wall. Several times within the hour and throughout the working day it sounded out like John Peel's hunting horn, "Telephone call for "X" in the Paint Shop! Telephone call for "X" in the Paint Shop!" It was a situation where a mobile telephone would have been an improvement and a blessing. Whitsuntide, with its flower and well dressing festivals were next to be violated by the local Mafia. They claimed the next door Roman well and sabotaged the harmony and peace that had prevailed. I counted at least seventeen Vicarage burglaries; one of these occurred in the small hours of morning. The burglars disturbed our sleep and escaped with all the garden statues; most precious was a sundial in memory of Joanna.

We are promised that the gates of Hell cannot prevail against the rock on which Heaven is built! We put this to the test and were not disappointed; although under siege, the Vicarage remained a haven of contentment and joy.

I named the cat next door, 'Edward Longshanks', after one of the best English Kings. This unfortunate and unhappy cat also seemed to have been created rather than begotten. He did not have the quintessence of perfection which is the hallmark of things evolved and fashioned by the Divine. He appeared as if he had been designed in the children's game when different children draw different parts of an animal in turn. One draws the head and folds the paper over: then the neck, the body, legs, tail and paws. In a nutshell "Edward Longshanks" emerged from the Old Vicarage ridiculously disproportionate. Such long legs are appropriate on a giraffe and very desirable on the right human being, but not on a white suitor for Koshka.

Edward Longshanks – 'Caught Red-Handed'

"Edward Longshanks" was caught red-handed with a live goldfish from the Vicarage pond; that was forgivable as the fish was injured! What was unforgivable was his lack-lustre un-catlike nature. However, love is blind and Koshka sat just looking at him under the coniferous trees amongst the daffodils which grew thickly in the rockery. Had she not been interfered with by the veterinary surgeon then there might have been a complete dynasty or a colony of "Koshka-Longshanks!"

No matter what happened to us or what threatened our peace, tranquillity never left us alone. When the Scrabble Board was produced every evening, that was the signal for Koshka to take up her favourite position in the armchair on Barbara's right side. She seemed to be engrossed and registered disagreement or her playfulness by raising her snow-white paw and gently moving the occasional letter. Whenever the record of 'The World of Your Hundred Best Tunes, vol.3" was played, she was enraptured. She purred her way through: The William Tell Overture and Tales from the Vienna Woods until Kathleen Ferrier sang, "Blow the Wind Southerly" then she could hardly contain herself! When Barbara sometimes whistled or joined in to sing "Blow the Wind Southerly" then Koshka's ecstasy was most obvious. She would roll on her back and expose her pure white underside as her alert ears and hazel eyes showed abandoned adoration. We were all taken into the realms expressed in the climax of the Liturgy by the words, "With angels and archangels and the whole company of

Heaven" and the timeless "Trisagion" (The Holy, Holy, Holy) of a glimpse of a greater reality.

CHAPTER 8

CUPBOARD LOVE

Some little boys seem to have the uncanny ability to see through refrigerator doors. On one occasion I had stocked the refrigerator with Fishermen's Friends and an assortment of menthol cough sweets when Paul, who had just come from school asked, "What are those sweets doing in the fridge, Granddad?" Although I wondered how he had time to learn their whereabouts I told him they were very nasty and only for old people with bad coughs. At three o'clock in the morning the bedroom door opened and Paul stood there coughing. "Jump into bed and cuddle up to Granddad!" I said, fearing that I should totally wake up. Paul was still for a minute or two and simulated, what he thought was a good coughing attack.

"Shall I have to stay in bed all tomorrow with a bad cough like this?" he asked. I assured him that was really on the cards. "Will I have to miss breakfast?" "Will I have to miss lunch?"

"Will I have to miss tea?" He punctuated his questions with a well-timed cough. "Of course!" I replied, "now snuggle down and go to sleep." He was deeply silent and summoning his punchline said, "Then I better have a packet of sweets and go to school!"

In the old days when Heaven and Earth were closer together and refrigerators had hardly been invented, my mother had a special relationship with her jet black cat called Smuts. She was cynical about all love-relationships; she saw all of them as expressions of Cupboard Love. Smuts was named after the famous General Smuts who worked for co-operation in the Commonwealth and the World. My father said that he was a good man, so my mother showed the cat considerable deference. When she had a few minutes break from attending to the demands and needs of her six children, or the field, the garden, the chickens, the pigs or the family business, she spoiled Smuts. She took great delight in buying lights from the butcher as a special treat. You always knew when she boiled lights (the lungs of sheep, pigs or bullocks), as the smell was obnoxious, but it drove Smuts crazy until the last morsel had been eaten. Although my mother was famous for saying, "I don't know what is the matter with that cat! He is always hungry! I fed him two weeks ago!" Smuts was well-satisfied and had a shiny black coat to prove it. He, like Kipling's "Cat that walked Alone", more than kept his part of the bargain; he not only caught mice but killed rats regularly and bit off their heads, displaying them by the soft-water butt by the kitchen door.

T.S. Eliot in his "The Addressing of Cats" says:

> "Before a cat will condescend
> To treat you as a trusted friend,
> Some little token of esteem
> Is needed like a dish of cream;
> And you might now and then supply
> Some caviar, or Strasbourg Pie,
> Some potted grouse, or salmon paste –
> He's sure to have his personal taste.
> (I know a Cat, who makes a habit
> Of eating nothing else but rabbit,

And when he's finished, licks his paws

So's not to waste the onion sauce.)

A Cat's entitled to expect

These evidences of respect."

Timmy, our Erlestoke episcopal cat was content with such brands as 'Whiskers', 'Kittycat' and 'Felix' but he supplemented his diet with a baby rabbit or two. He always showed his manners by leaving just one leg! Koshka liked white meats and disliked darker beef combinations. She was content with sardine or salmon flavours but not when there was a hint of freshly-cooked chicken about! Like Paul she also seemed to be able to look through closed refrigerator doors. She would go on hunger strike until she had begged and consumed the last remains of Sunday dinner.

CHAPTER 9

THE LAST SUPPER

The time came when Paul and Simon had to leave the Vicarage and say goodbye to us, Koshka and Derby. On a Wednesday evening Paul said to Grandma, "Sit down Grandma!" Barbara immediately sat down in her special chair with its spring-loaded ejector seat. "Daddy will be all right! I will look after him". His expression was so adult as he faced returning to London to a flat he left nine months previously. The five year old epitomised courage and bravery.

On the Friday he was in command again. "Sit down Grandma!" This time Barbara obeyed him sitting at the large round white kitchen table. "Sit down Simon! Sit down Granddad!" he continued. We are going to have a service!"

After an appropriate pause he said, "The Lord be with you!" I managed to be as serious as the occasion demanded. "And also with you!" I replied with a measure of amazement. "We are going to sing hymn number 60." He announced as if he had been the celebrant at St. Paul's Cathedral. "Sing it Grandma!" Barbara responded brilliantly. "Sing it Granddad!" I echoed the refrain both musically and in extempore phrases.

"The Lord be with you!" Paul continued which called forth the only reply I could possibly make.

"We are going to pray", Paul solemnly proceeded.

A Simple prayer followed which went directly to the heart of the Almighty in the wings of its sincerity and brevity. Paul had asked for orange squash instead of his usual milkshake and with this in mind he passed his sandwich around the table. Simon added the words, "You must say 'The Body of Christ'!"

Koshka looked on as the children rehearsed their last Supper. Paul finally passed round his cup of orange with the

words, "Drink Grandma! Drink Granddad! Drink Simon!"
After a night's sleep they left for the East End of London.

My mother, who lived until she was ninety seven, often repeated, "The best time of your life is when you have got your children with you!" Her words echoed the words of Christ, "Out of the mouth of babes and sucklings thou hast perfected praise". (Matthew 21.16). As the car left with Paul, Simon and their father, the words of the Last Supper remained; "This is my blood which is shed for you. Do this in remembrance of me!" The blood shed on Calvary was the blood Joanna shed on Pritchard Street and somehow it was the blood which fell from Koshka's chin in pools of deepest red on the white tiles of the kitchen floor.

The Dog that sold his Soul for a Chocolate Drop

CHAPTER 10

CATS, DOGS AND PIGS

A saying attributed to Sir Winston Churchill although it plays to the gallery does not hide our out-of-joint relationship with the animal world and our basic ignorance of the cat:- "All dogs look up to you. All cats look down on you. Only a pig looks at you as an equal!"

One landlord of the Owl at Little Cheverell kept chocolate drops for visiting dogs and served them first before he would draw your pint of Wadsworths. This pathetic attempt to curry favour with the customers back-fired and inane doggy-talk replaced the real-ale-conversation. One Saturday evening a stylish couple walked into the pub, packed with punters followed by a walking leash. The landlord and his wife drew the gaze of the crowded bar to the end of the lead. The nervous miniature dog was overcome by fear and confusion and piddled itself! Dogs do look up to us but at what a cost to the dog!

By selective breeding and canine connivance man has gained the upper hand in Creation to wield incalculable powers to hurt and destroy. The noble wolf did not so much as put on 'sheeps clothing' but he was humiliated and turned into a dog (not just the working or hunting dog to aid human imperialism but a liquorice-all-sorts of distortions such as sausage dogs, poodles and other refined mongrels just to puff up human vanity).

We celebrated the thousandth year of the Russian Orthodox Church by visiting Zagorsk, Moscow, St. Petersburg and the wonderful museums of those great cities. One of the abiding images which haunts my mind is a magnificent painting of the Last Great Assize.

The artist showed the world in it final stage from the animals point of view. In the dock was humankind with his accomplice the dog. Lions, elephants and other animals sat as judge and jury. Needless to say, the verdict was guilty. Both man and dog were together hanged.

In these days when we have the benefit of hindsight and the experiences of B.S.E. and foot and mouth disease there is a growing tendency to see our carnivorous appetite in much the same way as earlier generations viewed cannibalism. There are already signs that the wolf might be returned to the wilderness. As for the more ill-treated and much maligned pig there is talk of letting him out of his sty to roam our woodlands with the dignity that he once had as a 'wild boar'. Then, and only then, will he look at us as an equal.

Cats do not look down on us, for they are intelligent enough to know who can be trusted. To look into Koshka's gentle all-knowing eyes was to meet yourself as you really were and you could read the atmospheric conditions which prevailed in the household. Cats do not look down on us; they are like the barometer in the hall. They have a genius for discernment and indicate and measure with delicate accuracy the arbitrariness of our condition.

Even though Koshka enjoyed the normally relaxed atmosphere of the Vicarage she absented herself instantly when my voice was raised and she disappeared to the sound of the flapping cat flap. On another occasion Koshka showed her sensitivity and her dislike for a house-sitter who made herself equally unpopular; she fled the room rather than endure a moment more of over-indulgence.

Barbara, on the other hand, seemed to have inherited her ability to relate to cats through her father; he had a natural affinity with cats. He called then 'Tussas' or 'Pussy Cat Williams'. While her mother did not enjoy that blessed harmony which exists between cats and cat-lovers. When Tom, her husband, died, she unfortunately had a pedigree Siamese wished upon her to fill the gap. The cat was doubly unfortunate with his name; she called him 'Tiny'. No self-respecting Siamese would answer to 'Tiny'; he was most unhappy. In a most un-cat-like manner he preferred obscurity rather than being noticed and well-known. He spent his time avoiding people and hid shivering under the protection of the nearest bed.

The Egyptians placed the cat on a pedestal and in that

position Sir Winston's observation was literally true. But when a number of mummified cats were discovered in an Egyptian temple their resting place was unceremoniously violated. It was reported that an Englishman transported them back to Liverpool to be crushed and sold for fertiliser on the Wirral.

Cats scorn every human attempt to curtail their freedom as T S Eliot observed in his 'Rum Tum Tugger':-

"The Rum Tum Tugger is artful and knowing.
The Rum Tum Tugger doesn't care for a cuddle;
But he'll leap on your lap in the middle of your sewing.
For there's nothing he enjoys like a horrible muddle.....
For he will do
As he will do
And there's no doing anything about it!"

CHAPTER 11

BARBARA'S CAT

My mother judged people on how they got on with animals; if there was so much as a hint that you did not like cats then you 'cat-egorized' yourself as being less than one hundred per cent. By applying that criterion Barbara qualified as being on the side of angels. She and cats just got on. When we were sitting by the Sea of Galilee all sorts of cats spotted her and knew instinctively that they had a friend. While some cats sat by the water's edge trying to steal fish before the fisherman could catch them others hid themselves discretely amongst the restaurant tables. The cats did not utter a single meow nor was there any fighting for food. They were so quiet and imperceptible that they escaped the notice both of customer and management. They looked up at Barbara and patiently accepted the scraps although they were obviously starving.

As a little child she had a much-loved cat which was

also called Timmy. He, too, turned out to be a 'she' which she proved by having kittens. This young mother was run over to boost the statistics of fatal road accidents. All the Vicarage cats were firstly Barbara's cats, as was pre-eminently the first Timmy, the 'Bishop'. When the family walked to Erlestoke Post Office Timmy chose the safer route through the adjoining gardens skirting the parish. He waited by the telephone kiosk on Lower Road for his mistress to return home. He liked to accompany the family on outings to pick blackberries in the fields beyond the glebe.

On one occasion Timmy helped himself to an unfinished birthday cake, which did not diminish his popularity; rather enhanced it. Barbara had made Joanna a chocolate cake and left it on the sideboard while she fetched marzipan, icing sugar and candles.

Timmy missed this outing to the village shop preferring to stay at home and sample the cake. He made a large hole in the top. Barbara disguised the damage with icing and Joanna told her playmates what the cat had done. They, did not consider it an offence and devoured what remained.

Koshka's nearness to Barbara was evident when St. Paul's music group had their monthly rehearsal at the Vicarage. Tricia on clarinet and saxophone; Christopher on violin and cello; Margaret, the church organist, with her portable electronic organ and Gabrielle, the soloist. Koshka with the air "I would not miss this for the world" made herself comfortable and snuggled up close to Barbara. Margaret was an animal person: she definitely preferred George – her wolf-like Alsation – to the children she had to teach; she also more readily related to Koshka than to people. Maybe my mother was right to assess folk on how they got on with the animal-world!

Perhaps there is hope to be had in the idea that Paradise is not so much a lost condition but a quality of life yet to be discovered. If hell is just a temporal destructive force then heaven is eternal and transforms, transfigures and puts together all the broken pieces of our existence. The great thinkers of three thousand years ago saw that we were created to be park-keepers; our timeless pre-occupation is to care and be responsible for not just each other but for all things and creatures no matter how small.

CHAPTER 12

KOSHKA - MORE THAN A CAT

I used to play golf with a man whose name I just could not remember amongst the hundreds with whom I came into contact daily. But I could remember that he was 'an artificial inseminator of cows'. Once upon a time, when we were not so exposed to quantities of people, names had meaning and were memorable. They were keepsakes and vehicles of recognition. T S Eliot even made fictitious cats come to life by giving then fitting names:- 'Growltiger; Rum Tum Tugger; Mongojerrie and Rumpleteazer; Old Deuteronomy; Mr Mistofelees; Shimbleshanks and not forgetting the notorious Macavity!'

Koshka was born to worship; as the great hymn put it she was 'lost in wonder, love and praise'. She portrayed the adoration which the Great Masters capture in their timeless art and which you most experience in the Orthodox Church. Her presence in Derby made you feel as if you were in the monastery garden of St. Neophytus by Kato Paphos, Cyprus. The very name Koshka was a charm against racism (especially MaCarthyism), nationalism and all sorts of narrow-mindedness. As the Father of British history the Venerable Bede, used hyperbole when he wrote about the Emerald Isle so it is right to exaggerate about the name Koshka: "No snake can exist there; for although often brought over from Britain, as soon as the ships near the land, they breathe its scented air, and die".

I had asked an elderly retired priest how he viewed Derby before we had decided to move. He spoke of the then Bishop as being 'lower than the floorboards'. He must have been low for the Reverend Burnley was both comparatively low and a charitable man. However, Derby's problems were many and they were not all due to the Bishop's Churchmanship or lack of it. Derby Cathedral came into being as late as 1927, with dire consequences for its closest neighbour St. Paul's. As a stone thrown into a pond causes ripples to the furthermost shore, so the creation of this new ecclesiastical centre had far-reaching consequences for Derbyshire. The wonderful mediaeval church where the great Dr. Johnson had been married was turned into a shopping precinct; the living of St. Paul's was suspended and annexed to the new Cathedral. St. Paul's, already abandoned but for the very small residue of a handful of faithful worshippers, soon fell into disrepair. It stood black in the centre of Chester Green covered with a century's industrial pollution.

St. Paul's small parish had lost seventy five of its sons in the First World War and twenty six in the Second. After the wars some of the strongest families were moved wholesale to the new housing estate at Chaddesden. As if these happenings were not enough 'they' closed down St. Paul's school to create lasting bitterness.

One good thing occurred in this otherwise chapter of disasters: a much-loved retired bishop moved into the sub-standard new Vicarage. Bishop Parfitt had that rare quality we call 'holiness' which never totally deserted this ancient part of Derby.

By the Vicarage there are the remains of a Roman Mansio; the Inn of New Testament times. It is wonderful to imagine the travellers from far and wide resting there in the first Christian century – did one of the holy apostles penetrate this heart of England? I like to think that one did and this lends weight to the Scriptural promise that "In my Fathers house are many mansions. I go to prepare a place for you!" Although abused as this part of Derby has been there is something which haunts the area that is suggested in the indefinable word 'holy'.

My main work as Chaplain to Rolls-Royce and Bishop's Advisor to Industry was to allow a little sunshine into other dark corners of the City. St. Paul's was like Toad Hall when Toady had gone to gaol and a group of undesirable other creatures had taken control. It seemed that I was to let things fall into a state of greater dereliction and just go through the motions of keeping the life supports in place. In a period of ten years we restored St. Paul's; we sandblasted the building, re-pointed the brickwork, stripped the pitch-pine pews, renovated the oak doors, church clock, kneelers and chairs. Connachers rebuilt the organ and Rolls-Royce apprentices made and replaced the single strands of electrical cable with purpose-designed chandeliers. The work was recognised and won 'A BETTER CITY AWARD' for improving the environment.

Disaster then struck again. Prior to my arrival the small group which had taken control discovered dry rot! Instead of dealing with the problem they patched it up with hardboard and covered it with a lush red carpet.

Those who were responsible for and victims of this ultimate disaster applied to the Ecclesiastical Insurance for help; the insurance policy did not cover dry rot. Love covers many sins but hardboard and a red carpet can never hide deception for all time. When the hideous fungus appeared in the pulpit after ten years of restoration, I read from the expression of a prominent member the cruel secret that had been deliberately kept from me. In spite of the application for help from the Ecclesiastical Insurance Co. those-in-the-know put their hands on their hearts to disclaim all knowledge of the dry rot – they even said it did not exist!

In the Period of ten years we restored St Paul's Church.

'Lower than the floorboards' was prophetic indeed. We had an extraordinary meeting with the less-than-real Diocesan Committee for the Care of Churches which proved literally mind-blowing for me.

At crack of dawn in the mists of daylight on the next morning I teed off from the first at Horsley Lodge. The ball which normally went two hundred yards just trickled to my right. I repeated the shot with the same results. I found myself leaning on the back of my car struggling to change out of my spiked golf shoes. I drove home in the wrong gear and my foot felt as if it had turned into church lead.

Barbara quickly perceived I was not fooling around this time. I found myself in the strong arms of a Yorkshire paramedic who repeated "Ee you're a big lad John!" As I laid on the stretcher I felt my speech and the use of my right arm and leg diminished. I had had a Severe stroke.

Not only did Barbara have to contend with my predicament; the whole weight of the parish fell on her arthritic shoulders.   Koshka watched over the imperilled household. These were extraordinary circumstances; the bedroom which was normally strictly out of bounds became in bounds. I was safely in hospital and Koshka stretched herself full length on my side of the bed as if she were human; her cheeks caressed and comforted Barbara during those long and difficult nights.

CHAPTER 13

DRY ROT

Barbara and Koshka held the fort and kept each other company. The days were even busier with comings and goings at the Vicarage, there was a constant stream of visitors, with the relentless ringing of the door bell and the telephone. There were important meetings, church arrangements and the daily visits to the Derby Royal Infirmary; Barbara was more than glad to put her head down on her pillow with her little friend's reassuring closeness.

Dry rot had been growing insidiously throughout the church and had penetrated far lower than the floorboards; the builders had to act swiftly and dig several feet below to the very foundations. St. Paul's looked as if it had been hit by two bombs. Rolls-Royce responded in a practical way by taking some of the responsibility off Barbara's shoulders; they sent in their contractors to hang massive screens to close off the nave, the chancel, sanctuary and the tower, thus allowing the already-made arrangements for the Flower Festival to go ahead and the church to carry on functioning.

In hospital I sat trying to pick up plastic children's bricks of different shapes to place them in their respective receptacles. It was also difficult to cut up my food and find my mouth. I felt like a burglar, safe under the protection of the law. Things were far beyond my control and I laughed and laughed in the security that I was, for the time being, out of the range of my enemies. The hospital was amazed by my laughter and the consultant said my attitude had greatly assisted my recovery.

It was my sixty first birthday; I had celebrated it on 11 April until I was twenty and had to produce my birth certificate on being selected for ordination. It read 10 April 1934. I asked my mother how this difference had come about and she in her usual Solomonic way informed me that it was quite simple; I was born at midnight. So now I have two birthdays; one on the tenth and the other on the eleventh of April. On the 10 April the doctor said that he was so pleased with my progress that he was willing to let me go home whenever I wanted to. So I shared my good fortune with all my fellow patients and gave them my flowers, sweets, chocolates, grapes and other fruit and both my lemon and orange squash. They were slightly annoyed by my celebrations in particular as I repeatedly sang, "I....go....'ome.... t'morrow..." Unbeknown to me Barbara for very good reasons had asked the hospital to keep me in as long as possible for my own good.

I was immensely confused when the sister and the staff nurse spoke to me as if I were a naughty little boy, "Mr Lee", they said, "You are not going home tomorrow!" I telephoned the Vicarage and asked Barbara, "Why don't you want me to come home?" She replied, in a complete state of tearful exhaustion, "Come home if you want to. I can't stop you!" She replaced the receiver. I rang again to no avail. The study was a long way away from the lounge and besides the television when it was on blocked out every other sound. Then I started to worry that perhaps Barbara had fallen over. The combination of my inability to speak and sister's attitude meant that my predicament remained unsolved.

It was necessary to go to the Vicarage and ascertain whether or not all was well. So I slipped down the several flights of stairs to the foyer of the Royal Infirmary Hospital and the duty porter phoned up and ordered a taxi for me. I felt like a real escapee dressed in my pyjamas and no taxi fare. Apparently most of the hospital saw me escape and Barbara was instantly informed that there was a loose vicar on the run. When I was reassured that everything was all right, I kissed Barbara and patted Koshka and returned to my ward. On the 11 April, my second birthday, I asked some of my fellow sufferers for a glass of lemon squash which they gave me with a look of total disbelief.

CHAPTER 14

RECOVERY

In Seend, when I was the Vicar, we had a parishioner called Maisie who should be remembered because of her goodness. One kind act that Maisie did was to rescue a dog that had only half a stomach because he had been brutally kicked; he shivered in fear when humans approached. Maisie nursed the dog and fed him on a diet of chicken and he recovered to the point that outwardly he looked quite normal. It needs to be said that looking normal is by no means being normal. It is amazing to experience human kindness and consideration when you push someone in a wheelchair; the helping hand that is so willingly available in such circumstances seems to have been withdrawn when the wheelchair is removed. The disabled person is more vulnerable without the chair and the hand that would have held a door open lets it swing in the victim's face.

The hospital judged me to have made a ninety-five percent recovery; as wonderful as this was I would never be the same again. Besides the effects of the stroke there is the ageing process to take into consideration. Koshka, too was in the late Summer of her life. She could no longer leap up the eight foot garden wall with the agility that she had had; the spring had been diminished in her legs and she was becoming old. Barbara and I, although settling down to a four year period of ministry, had to consider moving from the resting place in Derby and listen to the voice that beckons all its children to come nearer home.

I sat on the Vicarage lawn with a senior colleague who had obviously imbibed how good it was to be there. His conversation at first was a eulogy which pleased me so much that I nodded in agreement at every word he uttered: Lovely garden! Nice House! Great Parish! Fine Church! Wonderful Job! Then the monologue took a subtle twist and concentrated on retirement. My retirement. As the conversation continued about retirement I sat listening without a word in silent disbelief of all that I was hearing. I thought how, when Joanna had been killed, that there seemed to be a plague of counsellors needing to counsel Paul and Simon. It seemed to me then that Paul and Simon were in a unique situation vis-à-vis the loss of their mother and should have been allowed to say how it was with them; in the same way I should have been given a chance to get a word in edgeways about my retirement. However, on 2 October in the same year I holed in one at Horsely Lodge Golf Club. Also by the assistance of the unchanging words of the great Church's liturgy I was able to sing, "Oh Lord open Thou our Lips" which was followed directly, "And our mouths shall show forth Thy praise". "Oh Lord open Thou our Lips". And thank God He did.

Retirement

CHAPTER 15

IN MY FATHER'S HOUSE
ARE MANY MANSIONS

The parish of St. Paul's flourished and quality buildings replaced the dereliction of St. Mary's Wharf. The relationship of Church and Industry was especially good. We raised an extra twelve thousand pounds to pay for the damage caused by the dry rot. Marelius Lacrymens – dry rot – thrives on poor ventilation and dampness; the fungus was in the pulpit and it had to be burned. Success inevitably highlights the dark areas of failure and neglect; stories were invented that the Vicar had sold the pulpit to the Americans and was retiring to Surrey on the proceeds.

I had not thought of retiring until I was seventy but it became obvious that my health was giving way under greater pressures. I calculated that if I stayed on for another five years, without doing anything else, I would have to conjure two hundred thousand pounds out of thin air; I would be like the miller's daughter in the story of Rumplestilzkin – she had to spin gold out of straw to save her baby.

We considered many options – retirement homes – and one of the deciding factors that influenced our choice was the nearness to our grandchildren. Paul had whispered the secret that he had learned, "If you lived nearer London then we would be allowed to see you more often," Eventually we settled for a bungalow built in Japanese style idyllically situated in the village of Churt; the place where Lloyd George's mistress had chosen for the great Prime Minister. The village is situated six miles from Farnham which is fifty minutes by train from Waterloo.

The only problem we encountered when we prepared to move from Derby was when we discovered the clause "NO PETS". Poor dear Koshka! We looked at the dilemma from all angles; we hoped the proper answer would come up during the twelve months prior to our move. Perhaps Koshka could remain as the 'Vicarage Cat' or perhaps one of the kind parishioners would adopt her.

Koshka was becoming an old lady, which was only detectable in the slower movements; her beautiful face never aged. It was the wrong time for her to move. The attachment of a cat to its home environment was illustrated to me by a man called Lawrence in the golf club. Lawrence and his family had moved four miles from Frensham to Farnham in Surrey. One of his cats immediately went missing. A few weeks went by and the resident in the old Frensham home telephoned Lawrence with the good news that the lost cat had just walked in through the cat flap. The cat had negotiated the outskirts of Farnham and picked his way through fields and villages to be where he wanted to be – home!

Barbara asked one of the committee members of the trust which oversaw the running of our future home in Surrey whether or not Koshka could finish her last years with us. The answer was "NO"; it would set a precedent and be a lever for those who were campaigning to have dogs. So she advertised for a good home in the Churt area and posted Koshka's photograph on the village shop notice board; Koshka was in a pose of sensuous adoration and showed her snow-white underside. As Jesus had found no place to be born in Bethlehem, so we were pleased that no one offered a home for this special cat. It was suggested that the old folk at Hindhead at 'Springkell' might benefit from the friendship of a cat. The matron interviewed us and assured us that at Koshka's time of life she should be with us.

We fixed our retirement date on 3 June 1999, Joanna's birthday, and actually moved on the fourteenth. The removal men came very early. Koshka was safely shut away in the large cupboard under the stairs, I was catching the fish and putting them into large blue tubs which my friend at the garden centre gave me and Barbara was doing many things at once. Koshka was put in a cat box and there were clear signs that "travelling along in an automobile" was anathema to her.

On our arrival Barbara took Koshka into the front garden where she sniffed around very cautiously and disappeared up a tree. Barbara sat down on a chair in the garden and Koshka settled down immediately. From the beginning she made herself scarce, instinctively keeping a low profile or remaining close at Barbara's side. She carefully explored the neighbourhood and found the open door at No.2 irresistible and inviting. Sybil, the ninety year occupant, exclaimed in indignant horror, "You should not be here!" Sybil was a stickler for obeying the qualifications for membership in the community. Apart from Koshka being a cat, she had the right credentials and fulfilled the required criteria for being in the community. She was 'The Vicarage Cat' par excellence; a real daughter of the Anglican Church with leanings to Orthodoxy in matters of worship. When the elderly Roddi, the deputy warden, was surprised by the stowaway Koshka she turned a blind eye; as if she were Nelson at the Battle of Trafalgar clapping his telescope to his sightless eye when confronted by the Armada and declaring "I'm blowed if I can see anything!"

As time went by Koshka won her way into the heart and hearts of the community; they understood that we were looking for a good home for a very valuable person. Koshka, as if aware of the delicate nature of her position, behaved with the highest degree of discretion. She was to be found sleeping under the smaller shrubs by ornamental garden walls or contented under the mauve, red and white rhodadendra behind our bungalow. At half-term and in the school holidays she was happy to be reunited with Paul and Simon; Simon gave her his old reassuring kiss. Koshka waited daily for our home-coming and escorted us inside the bungalow.

CHAPTER 16

CAMELLIA – AN EVERGREEN

Camellia is an evergreen shrub which like Christ came to us from Eastern Asia. I first met the name when I met the daughter of Peggy Coddrington, a lady from Seend who came with us on two pilgrimages to the Holy Land. Camellia was a beautiful young woman and a mother who was also taken from this life in a car accident. Through the gate, behind the garden wall the shrub camellia thrives. As the magnolia convinces one of the great artist behind Creation so does the camellia pose the questions, "Where did such a wonderfully-made flower come from? Why such fragility and for whose pleasure was it created?" The magnolia bloom takes us to the door of belief and the camellia takes us right into Gethsemane; the pink and deep red blooms fall like rings of precious sweat from the Saviour's head on the lawn.

At No.3 Eddystone Court Koshka had adjusted herself to this ready-made paradise. The wicker basket that she spurned in

Derby became her favourite bed and she took to eating and sleeping in the smaller toilet. Her freedom was curtailed, as there obviously was no cat flap. She definitely missed the comfort of Barbara's spring-loaded chair but made herself at home; sometimes lying sphinx-like with her white paws folded like a model pupil in an elite academy. She continued to take great interest in the evening game of Scrabble and occasionally she raised her snow-white paw to move a tile. She enjoyed her regular treat of the William Tell Overture – Finale and was enraptured by Kathleen Ferrier's singing "They told me last night that there were ships in the offing And I hurried down to the deep rolling sea".

When we went away, Koshka had to take full board and lodgings at the local cattery where she was well-known. She acquitted herself with great dignity like a dowager aristoC-r-A-T. The spring suddenly went from her legs but, although less agile, she retained something of that angelic prettiness which is in all newly-born animals. She showed her pain by stretching herself full length by the radiator rather than sitting as close as possible to Barbara. She was ill with deep heaving of her white flanks and showed her little pink half-tongue as she gasped. The vet at Beacon Hill at first seemed very brusque and kept Koshka in his animal hospital to observe in a more settled state. The next day he showed himself in his real colours as an unusually kind caring man. He had gone to Sainsbury's late to get some prawns to entice Koshka to eat. He informed us, "I wouldn't be beat!"

We took Koshka home where she neither ate nor improved. She was diagnosed as having "neutraphilia" and she showed signs of the disease by taking a long, long drink from the edge of the fish pond. We had to take her back to the vet and make a decision about her as we were going to Portugal. The vet consulted with his staff while Barbara administered the last pill. In spite of fussy boisterous dogs Koshka behaved with stoicism. Barbara and I agreed that for Koshka "the dark should be switched on". We wept.

The vet put Koshka in a cardboard box to carry her home.

Although we had told no one in the community about what had happened somehow everybody seemed to know. A neighbour sympathised and Paul, the administrator, was unusually present and told us that he would put it to the Trust Committee that cats might be a blessing to the community in the future.

Barbara and I buried Koshka close to our bungalow with words of the Authorised Prayer Book silently going through my mind:

"We commit Koshka's body to the earth in sure and certain hope of Resurrection to eternal life through out Lord Jesus Christ; who shall change this body of our low estate that it may be like unto his glorious body, according unto the mighty working, whereby he is able to subdue all things to himself."

CHAPTER 17

"WHO SWITCHED THE DARK ON?"

A lady who ran a cats rescue home for 85 unwanted ageing cats raised money for her project at Peterborough Antique Fair. On one occasion she was confronted by a very well-dressed bejewelled farmer's wife who refused to support the cause because , as she claimed, "I support many different sorts of animals!" The cat-carer was quick to reply, "Madame, it seems that many different sorts of animals support you!"

The excuse rings hollow and powerfully hypocritical in the light of what has happened in recent decades to what we used to call husbandry. The apocalyptic events caused by mad cows disease, the foot and mouth epidemic and the floods, aided and abetted by neglect and abuse of both farmland and rivers, give all but the most insensitive a foretaste of an impending hell. What is happening to our planet is happening to everyone and everything. Hell takes no prisoners; there is only one escape-route from its jaws. That is through Heaven's gate.

Koshka could have gone to live in her retirement to a cat's home which is situated by the pad where Rolls-Royce fly in VIPs by helicopter, but such a place would not have been ideal for our heroine. This cats home was the best that I have heard of; it comprises a converted house where the cats live upstairs in community and have free range of all the rooms including a play area. But as good as it is for abused cats it would have denied Koshka access to the greater world and that most important ingredient – an adjusting and adjusted relationship with her family.

Retirement is when we return to a condition when time does not exist; when the clock stops for ever on the factory gate and its tyranny over Life's prisoners is finally curtailed. Heaven is a timeless place where abuses are forgiven and wounds and scars are healed. It is returning to one's childhood when reality and daylight only ceases when the shutters on tired eyes are closed. Even then our experience deepens. As children we learned to close our eyes and fly on the wings of our imagination to cross the boundaries of space and time.

Karen, our three year old daughter, used to ask Barbara at bedtime, "Mummy, who switched the dark on?" In Churt there are no street lights. In this part of England, where Hampshire meets Surrey, human domination and despoliation has been limited; heathlands and woodlands still provide shelter for God's threatened creatures. It is imperative and urgent that we should "switch the darkness on!" The darkness where no wrong-doing and pollution are seen; the darkness that obliterates them and consigns them to the emptiness of Hells' dumping ground. In the "Lament for the Loss of Great Music", Hugh McDiarmid, the Scots poet, speaks of how a drought can heighten our perception and hearing. It is like switching "the dark on". He tells how in the stillness of a drought, he once heard a dipper's song; as the waters abated he thought at first it was the mavis. He comments, "We allow too little for the babbling Stream and the cascade's roar".

In my retirement as I walk home late at night I rejoice that someone had the forethought and foresight "to switch the darkness on".

Now I pause at the antique gate of our retirement complex and gaze as I did as a child at the velvet sky with its infinitude of planets and stars. Here, although threatened, the watchful darkness has its wise eyes as Gray in his Elegy writes:

"The moping owl does to the moon complain Of such as, wandering near her secret bower, Molest her ancient solitary reign"

When the friendly darkness is switched on, if we are blessed, we find ourselves once more enfolded in Nature's arms where the soothing song of the lullaby wakes us up and our dreams come true.

Behind the kind of lych-gate is a Mediaeval barn and lattice-windowed "Quinnettes" and Eddystone Court, built in the memory of the founder's father who was the Douglas who built the fifth and final Eddystone Lighthouse at Plymouth. The wall hides four acres of secret garden where the immaculate magnolias are rivalled by an equally spectacular dogwood blossom. The community was to have provided affordable accommodation for returning and retiring missionaries. In spite of the shortage of missionaries, Heaven has been allowed a small patch of Earth, where the beneficiaries, foxes, badgers and Koshka sleep by day when someone switches "the darkness on".

THE REVELATION OF ST. JOHN THE DIVINE

Revelation ch.21.

And I saw a new heaven and a new earth:
for the first heaven and the first earth were
passed away; and there was no more sea.

And I John saw the holy city, new
Jerusalem, coming down from God out of
heaven, prepared as a bride adorned for
her husband. And I heard a great voice
out of heaven saying, Behold, the
tabernacle of God is with men, and he will
dwell with them, and they shall be his
people, and God himself shall be with
them, and be their God.

And God shall wipe away all tears from
their eyes; and there shall be no more
death, neither sorrow, nor crying, neither
shall there be any more pain: for the
former things are passed away.
And he that sat upon the throne said,
Behold I make all things new.

The Author

The Reverend John Foden Lee A.K.C. Born 10 April 1934 in Northampton. Pupil of Spratton, C/E Primary School and Northampton Town and County School for Boys. Aged sixteen to eighteen was a bespoke and surgical shoemaker and managed a shoe repair shop in Luton, Beds.

1952-1954. National Service. R.A.F. Russian Linguist, Joint School for Linguists Coulsdon Common Camp, Surrey. Pre-ordination training in the Brewery Industry and Stewarts and Lloyds Corby (Steel).

1956-1962,William Temple College, Rugby; King's College, London University; St. Boniface College, Warminster.

Curate of All Saints and Christ the Carpenter, Peterborough.

Married Barbara Catherine Hutton, (Sunday School Teacher and Author of The Legacy, The Huttons of Beetham and Penrith).

Curacies St. Andrews, Sudbury Town, Wembley and Sherborne Abbey, Dorset.
1968-1979, Rector of Gt. Cheverell, Vicar of Erlestoke, Chaplain H.M. Prison, Erlestoke House, Wiltshire.

1979-1986, Vicar of Holy Cross Seend and Christ Church, Bulkington.

1986-1999, Bishop's Advisor to Industry, Chaplain to Rolls-Royce (Aero Engines) and Davis of Derby. Vicar of St. Paul's, Chester Green, Derby.

1999, Retired to Churt, Surrey.

Karen, married to Howard, the older daughter of John and Barbara, has three children; Ben, Harriet and Gregory.

Joanna married Philip and was killed on 14 October 1992 in the East End of London, leaving Paul and Simon.

Barbara and John have exchanged parishes in the U.S.A. Canada, and Norway. They are keen travellers and have led pilgrimages in the Holy Land.

Previous writings by the present author: 'After April when May Follows. . .' , 'The Apprentice (The Relic of St. Boniface)' and 'The Devil on a Leather Thong'.